For Product Safety Concerns and Information please contact our EU
representative GPSR@taylorandfrancis.com
Taylor & Francis Verlag GmbH, Kaufingerstraße 24, 80331 München, Germany

www.ingramcontent.com/pod-product-compliance
Ingram Content Group UK Ltd.
Pitfield, Milton Keynes, MK11 3LW, UK
UKHW041337160825
461941UK00023B/889

Thank You!

First and foremost, I would like to express my heartfelt gratitude to you, the reader. Thank you for choosing this book and taking the time to journey through the fascinating events, facts, and stories that shaped the world during the year 1996.

This book is dedicated to those who seek knowledge, celebrate the wonders of the past, and look forward to shaping a better future.

Table of Contents

1996

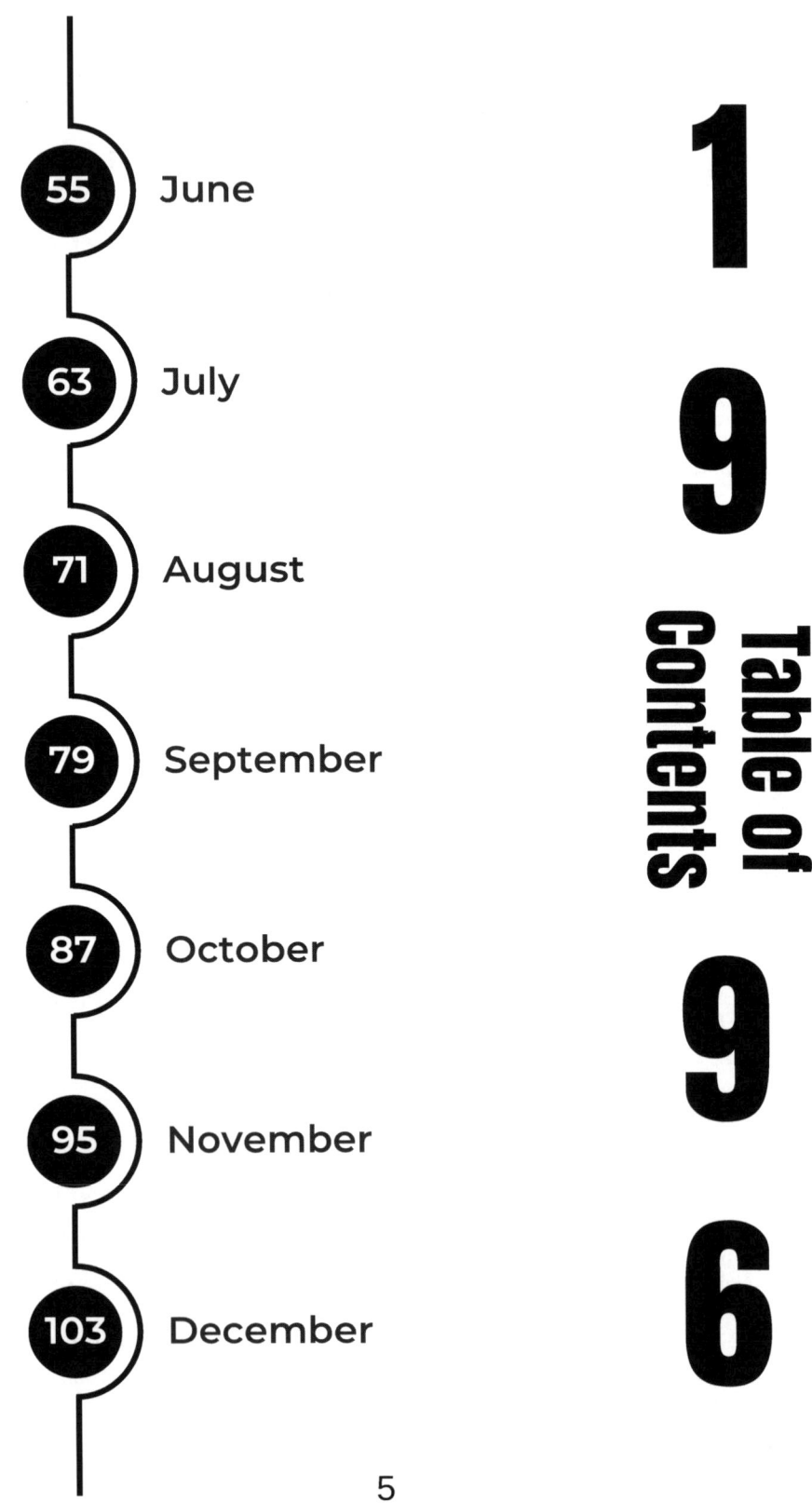

Table of Contents

1996

Triumph and Terror: A Summer of Celebration and Tragedy

The year 1996 was a year of profound and often jarring contrasts, a time when moments of immense national pride and global celebration were violently interrupted by acts of terror and inexplicable disaster. The United States hosted the world for the Centennial Olympic Games, a spectacle of athletic triumph that was tragically marred by a bombing. And even as the nation enjoyed a booming economy that would re-elect its president, it was forced to confront new fears and mourn stunning losses. It was a year that showcased both the heights of human achievement and the depths of human malice.

An American-Hosted Olympics and an Act of Terror

The world's attention turned to Atlanta, Georgia, for the 1996 Summer Olympics. The Games began with one of the most emotional and unforgettable moments in Olympic history. At the opening ceremony, the final torchbearer was revealed to be the legendary boxer

Muhammad Ali. Visibly shaking from Parkinson's disease, Ali bravely and defiantly lit the Olympic cauldron, a moment of immense courage and poignancy. The Games were filled with triumphant performances, from Michael Johnson's stunning, gold-medal sweep in the 200-meter and 400-meter races to the "Magnificent Seven" U.S. women's gymnastics team, whose victory was secured by Kerri Strug's heroic final vault on an injured ankle.

But the celebratory atmosphere was shattered in the early morning hours of July 27. A pipe bomb filled with nails and screws exploded in Centennial Olympic Park, a public space where crowds were gathered for a concert. The blast killed one person directly and caused the death of another from a heart attack, injuring over 100 more. The tragedy could have been far worse if not for the actions of security guard Richard Jewell, who discovered the suspicious backpack and helped to clear the immediate area. In a cruel twist, Jewell, initially hailed as a hero, was later wrongly named by the media and the FBI as the primary suspect, and was subjected to months of intense and unjust public scrutiny before being exonerated.

Tragedy Over the Atlantic: TWA Flight 800

Just ten days before the Olympic bombing, the nation was rocked by another shocking disaster. On July 17, TWA Flight 800, a Boeing 747 bound for Paris, exploded in mid-air shortly after taking off from New York's JFK Airport, killing all 230 people on board. The disaster, which occurred over the Atlantic Ocean off the coast of Long Island, immediately sparked fears of a terrorist attack, similar to the 1988 bombing of Pan Am Flight 103 over Lockerbie, Scotland. The long and difficult investigation would ultimately conclude that the cause was a fuel tank explosion sparked by faulty wiring, but the incident left a deep sense of vulnerability and fear.

The "Comeback Kid" Wins Again

The backdrop for these events was a booming American economy and a presidential election. President Bill Clinton, who had presided over a period of peace and growing prosperity, ran on the theme of "Building a Bridge to the 21st Century." He faced Republican challenger Senator Bob Dole of Kansas. On November 5,

Clinton won re-election decisively, becoming the first Democrat to win a second full term since Franklin D. Roosevelt.

A Scientific Milestone: Dolly the Sheep

A revolutionary scientific breakthrough occurred in a laboratory in Scotland, though the world would not learn of it until the following year. On July 5, Scottish scientists successfully cloned the first mammal from an adult cell, a sheep they named Dolly. The achievement would spark a fierce global debate about the ethics of cloning and its potential applications for humanity.

The Unabomber is Caught

One of the longest and most difficult manhunts in FBI history came to an end on April 3. Theodore "Ted" Kaczynski, known as the "Unabomber," was arrested at his remote, primitive cabin in Montana. For 17 years, Kaczynski had waged a mail-bombing campaign against universities and airlines, killing three people and injuring 23 more.

Conclusion: A Year of Conflicting Emotions

1996 was a year of deeply conflicting emotions. The pride and joy of the Atlanta Olympics were forever intertwined with the tragedy of the park bombing. The comfort of a strong economy was unsettled by disaster and new fears of terrorism. And a triumphant re-election for a president was set against a backdrop of national mourning and uncertainty. It was a year that demonstrated how quickly celebration can turn to tragedy, and how resilient a nation must be in the face of both.

Cost of living

The year 1996 was a time of significant economic prosperity and confidence in the United States. The "dot-com" boom was in full swing, the stock market was soaring, and unemployment was low. For many American families, with a median household income of over $35,000, it was a time of comfort and opportunity. The economic anxieties of the early part of the decade had largely faded, replaced by a sense of optimism fueled by a strong economy and a revolutionary new technology: the World Wide Web.

The internet was no longer a niche hobby for tech enthusiasts; it was going mainstream. The sound of a dial-up modem connecting was becoming a familiar household noise. Internet service providers like America Online (AOL) were signing up millions of new customers, offering them their first taste of email, chat rooms, and the Web. A new home personal computer, likely running the new Windows 95 operating system, was a major purchase at around $2,000, but was increasingly seen as an essential gateway to the new digital world.

This consumer confidence was on full display during the holiday season, which was dominated by a craze for one particular toy: Tickle Me Elmo. The giggling red doll became the must-have item of the year, leading to shopping frenzies and shortages across the country. In the world of video games, the "console war" heated up with the release of the new 64-bit Nintendo 64, which competed with the Sony PlayStation for dominance in living rooms. The cost of major purchases like a new car (around $20,500) or a new home (around $140,000) was substantial, but a strong economy and relatively low interest rates made them feel attainable for a growing middle class.

On the next page, you'll find a "**Cost of Living List**" & "**Cost of Living Comparison: 1996 vs. Today.**"

Income & Major Purchases (1996):
- Median Household Income: ~$35,492
- Minimum Wage: $4.75 per hour
- Median Home Price: ~$140,000
- Average Monthly Rent: ~$576
- New Car Price: Around $20,500

Groceries & Daily Essentials (1996):
- Loaf of Bread: $1.15
- Gallon of Milk: ~$3.15
- Dozen Eggs: $1.31
- Pound of Ground Beef: $1.42
- Gallon of Gasoline: ~$1.23

Entertainment & Leisure (1996):
- Movie Ticket: $4.42
- Newspaper: $0.50
- Music CD: ~$15.99
- Postage Stamp (First Class): $0.32
- Nintendo 64 Video Game: ~$199.99

Technology & Pop Culture (1996):
- Personal Computer: ~$2,000
- Tickle Me Elmo doll (retail): ~$28.99
- Dial-up Internet Service (AOL): ~$19.95 per month (for unlimited use)
- DVD Player (first models): ~$700+

Cost of Living Comparison: 1996 vs. Today

Category	1996	Today
Income & Home		
Median Household Income	~$35,492	$85,000 - $95,000
Median Home Price	~$140,000	$400,000 - $450,000
New Car Price	~$20,500	$40,000 - $50,000
Groceries & Gas		
Loaf of Bread	$1.15	$3.50 - $5.00
Gallon of milk	~$3.15	$4.00 - $5.50
Dozen eggs	$1.31	$3.50 - $5.50
Gallon of gas	~$1.23	$3.50 - $5.00
Entertainment & Tech		
Movie ticket	$4.42	$15 - $25
Postage Stamp	$0.32	~$0.70
Personal Computer	~$2,000	$600 - $2,500+
Internet Subscription	~$19.95/mo.	$50 - $100/mo.

Back to
January
History

January

S	M	T	W	T	F	S
	1	2	3	4	5	6
7	8	9	10	11	12	13
14	15	16	17	18	19	20
21	22	23	24	25	26	27
28	29	30	31			

1996

A New Declaration, A Monster Storm

January 1996 was a month where both the political and literal climates of the United States were dramatically altered. A monster blizzard of historic proportions buried the entire Eastern Seaboard, paralyzing the nation's most powerful cities and shutting down the federal government itself. And just a few weeks later, from the House chamber of that same government, the President of the United States made a stunning declaration that would fundamentally reshape the political landscape, announcing that "the era of big government is over."

The Blizzard of '96: The East Coast Shuts Down

From January 6 to 8, one of the most severe snowstorms in American history pummeled the East Coast. The Blizzard of '96 was a behemoth, dumping between two and four feet of snow on a vast area stretching from Washington, D.C., to Philadelphia, New York City, and Boston. The storm brought life to a complete standstill. Major airports were closed

for days, highways were impassable, and states of emergency were declared up and down the coast. The federal government in Washington was forced to shut down. The storm was responsible for more than 150 deaths and caused billions of dollars in economic damage, a powerful and humbling reminder of nature's ability to paralyze modern society.

"The Era of Big Government is Over": Clinton's Pivotal Speech

After the Republican Revolution of 1994, President Bill Clinton, a Democrat, faced a hostile Republican-controlled Congress and a tough re-election campaign. In his State of the Union address on January 23, he executed a brilliant political maneuver that would define his presidency. In a line that stunned many in his own party, Clinton declared, "The era of big government is over." He went on to embrace traditionally Republican issues like balancing the budget and reforming welfare. The speech was a masterclass in political "triangulation." By co-opting the core message of his opponents, Clinton repositioned himself as a pragmatic centrist, a "New Democrat" who was no longer

bound by the old liberal orthodoxies. The declaration was a pivotal moment that disarmed his critics and set him on a clear path to re-election.

A New Leader for Palestine

A key milestone in the Middle East peace process was reached on January 20. In the first-ever Palestinian general election, Yasser Arafat, the long-time chairman of the Palestine Liberation Organization (PLO), was elected President of the newly created Palestinian National Authority. The election, which took place in the West Bank and Gaza Strip, was a crucial step in implementing the Oslo Accords and creating a new governing body for the Palestinian people.

A Hostage Crisis in Chechnya

The brutal war in the Caucasus continued. On January 9, a large group of Chechen rebels launched a raid on the Russian city of Kizlyar in the neighboring republic of Dagestan. They seized a hospital and took an estimated 2,000 people hostage, demanding the withdrawal of Russian troops from Chechnya.

The crisis ended in a bloody and botched rescue attempt by Russian forces, resulting in many casualties.

Conclusion: A Change in the Weather

January was a month that saw a powerful demonstration of nature's ability to halt modern life, and a powerful demonstration of a politician's ability to adapt to a new political climate. The Blizzard of '96 was a temporary paralysis, but President Clinton's declaration that the era of big government was over would have a lasting impact, reshaping the political debate for years to come.

Back to January memories

....

....

....

....

....

....

....

....

....

Picture of the month

01/1996

Back to February History

February

S	M	T	W	T	F	S
				1	2	3
4	5	6	7	8	9	10
11	12	13	14	15	16	17
18	19	20	21	22	23	24
25	26	27	28	29		

1996

The End of a Ceasefire, The End of a Marriage, The Dawn of a New Intelligence

February 1996 was a month of significant and often painful endings that signaled a shift into a new, more complex era. In London, a fragile peace process was shattered by the return of terrorist violence. In the royal palaces, a modern fairy tale officially came to its sad conclusion. And in a quiet chess match in Philadelphia, a new kind of intelligence announced its arrival, as a human world champion was defeated by a machine for the very first time, a milestone that would have profound implications for the future.

Man vs. Machine: Kasparov vs. Deep Blue

The month's most intellectually significant event was a six-game chess match between the world's greatest player, Garry Kasparov, and an IBM supercomputer named Deep Blue. The match was a major test of the state of artificial intelligence. The chess world and the public were stunned on February 10 when, in the first

game of the match, Deep Blue defeated Kasparov. It was the first time in history that a computer had beaten a reigning world champion under standard tournament conditions. Kasparov, who was visibly unsettled by the computer's alien and unconventional moves, would later regroup and win the overall match 4-2. But the damage was done. The first game was the true landmark—the "John Henry" moment for the computer age. It proved that machine intelligence was rapidly advancing and that the day was coming when humanity would no longer be the undisputed master of its most celebrated intellectual game.

The Ceasefire is Over: The IRA Bombing of London

The hopeful peace process in Northern Ireland was shattered on February 9. A massive truck bomb, planted by the Provisional Irish Republican Army (IRA), exploded in the Canary Wharf financial district of London. The powerful blast killed two people, injured more than 100, and caused hundreds of millions of pounds in damage. The bombing officially ended a 17-month IRA ceasefire and marked a brutal return

to violence after a period of intense optimism and negotiation. The attack was a devastating setback for those who had worked to bring an end to "The Troubles."

The Final End of a Royal Marriage

The long, slow, and very public unraveling of the marriage of Prince Charles and Princess Diana reached its official conclusion. On February 28, a spokesperson for Diana announced that she had formally agreed to a divorce from the Prince of Wales, the heir to the British throne. The announcement was the final, sad end to the "fairy tale" marriage that had begun with a spectacular royal wedding in 1981. After years of scandal, media wars, and public unhappiness, the separation was inevitable, but the official confirmation was still a major moment, closing the book on one of the most famous and scrutinized relationships of the 20th century.

Conclusion: A Month of Endings

February was a month that felt like the end of many eras. The end of a truce in Northern Ireland signaled a return to a bitter conflict.

The end of a royal marriage closed a chapter on a public fascination. And the end of humanity's undisputed supremacy in chess signaled the beginning of a new and uncertain relationship between human and artificial intelligence. The month was a clear sign that the world was moving into a new and more complex phase, both in its political conflicts and its relationship with technology.

Back to February memories

....

....

....

....

....

....

....

....

....

Picture of the month

02/1996

Back to March History

March

S	M	T	W	T	F	S
					1	2
3	4	5	6	7	8	9
10	11	12	13	14	15	16
17	18	19	20	21	22	23
24	25	26	27	28	29	30
31						

1996

A Public Health Panic and a Military Standoff

March 1996 was a month of global anxiety. In the United Kingdom, a frightening new health crisis emerged as the government finally admitted a link between "Mad Cow Disease" and a fatal human illness, sparking a panic that would decimate the British beef industry. At the same time, in East Asia, a tense military standoff was brewing, as China used aggressive missile tests to intimidate Taiwan, prompting a major show of force from the United States. It was a month that highlighted the new and unpredictable dangers of the post-Cold War world.

"Mad Cow Disease": A Crisis in the UK

On March 20, the British government made a terrifying announcement that created a full-blown public health panic. After years of denying any link, health officials conceded that there was a probable connection between Bovine Spongiform Encephalopathy (BSE), a degenerative neurological disease in cattle known as "Mad Cow Disease," and a new, fatal

variant of Creutzfeldt-Jakob disease in humans. The news that eating beef could potentially lead to an incurable and fatal brain disease horrified the public. The British beef industry collapsed overnight. Schools stopped serving beef to children, and the European Union and countries around the world immediately banned all imports of British beef. The crisis would have a devastating economic and psychological impact on Britain for years.

A Standoff in the Taiwan Strait

The most serious military confrontation of the post-Cold War era was unfolding in the waters between China and Taiwan. In an attempt to intimidate voters ahead of Taiwan's first-ever direct presidential election, the People's Republic of China began a series of aggressive military exercises. This included firing M-9 ballistic missiles into the sea near Taiwan's two largest ports. The "missile diplomacy" was a blatant act of military bullying. The United States responded swiftly and forcefully. In a clear message to Beijing, President Clinton ordered two U.S. aircraft carrier battle groups into the region. The deployment was the largest

display of American military power in Asia since the Vietnam War and it successfully de-escalated the crisis, but not before a tense standoff that brought the two nuclear powers uncomfortably close to conflict.

The Race is Set: Bob Dole Becomes the Nominee

The race for the Republican presidential nomination effectively came to an end in March. With a string of victories in the major primaries, Senate Majority Leader Bob Dole of Kansas secured enough delegates to become the presumptive nominee. After a long and distinguished career in the Senate, Dole finally captured the prize he had sought for years. The general election matchup was now set: President Bill Clinton versus Senator Bob Dole.

A Rebel Yell at the Oscars

Hollywood celebrated the films of 1995 at the 68th Academy Awards on March 25. The big winner of the night was Mel Gibson's historical epic, Braveheart. The bloody tale of Scottish rebel William Wallace's fight for freedom against the English won five Oscars, including

the top two awards for Best Picture and Best Director for Gibson.

Conclusion: A Month of New Anxieties

March was a month that introduced the world to new anxieties. The fear of a mysterious and deadly disease from the food supply, and the fear of a new military conflict between major world powers, were both stark reminders that the end of the Cold War had not created a safer or more predictable world. Instead, it was a world of new, complex, and often frightening challenges.

Back to March memories

Picture of the month

03/1996

Back to
April
History

April

S	M	T	W	T	F	S
	1	2	3	4	5	6
7	8	9	10	11	12	13
14	15	16	17	18	19	20
21	22	23	24	25	26	27
28	29	30				

1996

The Loner's Rage: A Cabin in Montana, A Massacre in Tasmania

April 1996 was a month that brought two very different stories of isolated male rage to a shocking conclusion. In the mountains of Montana, one of the longest manhunts in American history came to a quiet end with the arrest of the Unabomber, while in Australia, a horrific mass shooting by a lone gunman plunged the nation into grief and led to a profound change in its society.

The Unabomber is Caught

For 17 years, he had been a ghost, a mysterious terrorist who mailed or delivered increasingly sophisticated bombs to universities and airlines, waging a one-man war against modern technology. The FBI's "UNABOM" case was one of its most expensive and frustrating. The breakthrough came from a desperate gamble. In 1995, the Unabomber had demanded that major newspapers publish his 35,000-word anti-technology manifesto, promising to stop the bombings if they did. The Washington Post and The New York Times

complied. The publication led to a tip from a man named David Kaczynski, who recognized the ideological arguments and turns of phrase in the manifesto as those of his estranged, reclusive brother, Ted. On April 3, 1996, FBI agents raided a tiny, primitive cabin in the mountains of Montana and arrested Theodore "Ted" Kaczynski, a former mathematics prodigy with a PhD from Harvard. The long reign of terror was finally over.

The Port Arthur Massacre

On April 28, the Australian state of Tasmania experienced a day of unimaginable horror. A 28-year-old man named Martin Bryant, armed with semi-automatic rifles, went on a shooting rampage at the historic Port Arthur tourist site. He opened fire in a café, a gift shop, and the surrounding grounds, killing and wounding people indiscriminately. By the time he was captured the next morning after a police standoff, he had killed 35 people and wounded 23 more. It was, and remains, the deadliest mass shooting in Australia's history. The massacre deeply shocked the Australian public and prompted a swift and powerful political

response. In the weeks that followed, the Australian federal and state governments worked together to enact strict, sweeping new gun control laws, including a ban on all semi-automatic rifles and a massive, mandatory gun buyback program.

War in Lebanon: Operation Grapes of Wrath

The Middle East saw another round of intense violence. On April 11, Israel launched a massive 16-day military offensive called Operation Grapes of Wrath against Hezbollah forces in southern Lebanon. The campaign involved heavy aerial bombing and artillery shelling. The offensive created a major international incident on April 18, when Israeli artillery shelled a United Nations compound at Qana, where hundreds of Lebanese civilians had taken shelter. Over 100 people were killed in the shelling, which Israel called a tragic error. The event drew widespread international condemnation and highlighted the devastating human cost of the conflict.

Conclusion: A Reckoning with Violence

April was a month that forced multiple nations

to confront the destructive power of alienated individuals. The capture of the Unabomber was the end of a long reign of terror, while the massacre in Australia was the shocking beginning of a national debate on gun violence. Both events, in their own way, were grim case studies in the destructive potential of a lone, alienated man.

Back to April memories

....

....

....

....

....

....

....

....

....

Picture of the month

04/1996

Back to May History

May

S	M	T	W	T	F	S
			1	2	3	4
5	6	7	8	9	10	11
12	13	14	15	16	17	18
19	20	21	22	23	24	25
26	27	28	29	30	31	

1996

Into Thin Air: Disaster on Everest and in the Everglades

May 1996 was a month defined by shocking and tragic disasters. On the treacherous slopes of the world's highest mountain, a deadly storm claimed the lives of experienced climbers in a high-altitude drama. And in the skies over Florida, a passenger jet plunged into the Everglades after a fire broke out on board, leaving no survivors. It was a month that served as a powerful and sobering reminder of the unforgiving power of nature and the devastating consequences of human error.

Death on the Roof of the World: The Everest Disaster

In the spring of 1996, a record number of climbers were attempting to summit Mount Everest. On May 10, several commercial and private expeditions made a push for the top, creating a "traffic jam" high up on the mountain. But as the climbers were descending from the summit, a sudden and ferocious blizzard struck. The storm trapped multiple teams in the "death zone" above 26,000 feet, with hurricane-force

winds and temperatures plunging far below zero. In the chaos and confusion that followed, eight climbers, including several renowned and experienced guides like Rob Hall and Scott Fischer, died from exposure and exhaustion. The 1996 Everest disaster, which would be famously chronicled in Jon Krakauer's bestselling book Into Thin Air, was one of the deadliest single events in the mountain's history and it sparked an intense debate about the commercialization of climbing the world's highest peak.

Fire in the Sky: The Crash of ValuJet 592

Just one day after the tragedy on Everest, another disaster unfolded in the United States. On May 11, ValuJet Flight 592, a DC-9 aircraft, took off from Miami bound for Atlanta. Shortly after takeoff, a fire broke out in the forward cargo hold. The fire was later found to have been caused by improperly stored and expired chemical oxygen generators, which are used to provide oxygen for passenger masks. The pilots struggled to control the burning aircraft as the cabin filled with smoke, but they lost control, and the plane plunged at a steep angle into the

Florida Everglades. All 110 people on board were killed instantly. The crash of the low-cost carrier's plane led to major reforms in airline safety regulations, particularly concerning the transport of hazardous materials on passenger aircraft.

A New Leader for Israel

The Middle East peace process, which had seen so much hope in recent years, faced a major new challenge. In the Israeli prime ministerial election on May 31, Benjamin Netanyahu, the leader of the right-wing Likud party, scored a narrow victory over the incumbent, Shimon Peres of the Labour Party. Peres had been one of the key architects of the Oslo Accords. Netanyahu had campaigned on a much tougher, more skeptical platform regarding the peace process. His election signaled a significant shift to the right in Israeli politics and created a new and uncertain future for negotiations with the Palestinians.

Conclusion: A Month of Tragedy

May was a month dominated by stories of

tragedy and loss. The disasters on Mount Everest and in the Florida Everglades were powerful reminders of human vulnerability in the face of nature and error. And the election of a new, more hardline government in Israel cast a shadow of doubt over the future of the Middle East peace process. It was a sobering month that tempered the optimism of the mid-1990s with a dose of harsh reality.

Back to May memories

....

....

....

....

....

....

....

....

....

....

Picture of the month

05/1996

Back to June History

June

S	M	T	W	T	F	S
						1
2	3	4	5	6	7	8
9	10	11	12	13	14	15
16	17	18	19	20	21	22
23	24	25	26	27	28	29
30						

1996

A Legendary Season, A Deadly Blast

June 1996 was a month that juxtaposed the thrill of ultimate sporting triumph with the shock of a deadly terrorist attack. In Chicago, a legendary basketball team capped off arguably the greatest single season in professional sports history, a story of unparalleled dominance and excellence. But halfway around the world, in the deserts of Saudi Arabia, a massive truck bomb brought tragedy and a new sense of vulnerability to the U.S. military. It was a month that saw both a team reach the pinnacle of its sport and a nation confront the brutal reality of terrorism.

The Greatest Team Ever? The Bulls Complete Their 72-10 Season

The 1995-96 season was a historic one for Michael Jordan and the Chicago Bulls. After returning from his brief retirement to play baseball, Jordan was on a mission to re-establish his dominance. The Bulls responded with a season for the ages, compiling a regular season record of 72 wins and only 10 losses, the best in NBA history up to that point.

They steamrolled through the playoffs and, on June 16, they defeated the Seattle SuperSonics to win their fourth NBA championship in six years. The championship was the triumphant culmination of a legendary season. It re-established Michael Jordan as the undisputed king of basketball and cemented the 90s Bulls' legacy as arguably the greatest basketball team ever assembled.

Terror in Saudi Arabia: The Khobar Towers Bombing

The celebratory mood in the U.S. was shattered on June 25. A massive truck bomb exploded outside the Khobar Towers, a high-rise housing complex in Dhahran, Saudi Arabia, which was being used to house American military personnel assigned to monitor a no-fly zone over southern Iraq. The bomb was enormous, estimated to be the equivalent of 20,000 pounds of TNT. The blast ripped the face off of one of the eight-story buildings, killed 19 U.S. Air Force servicemen, and injured nearly 500 other people. The attack, which was later attributed to Hezbollah Al-Hejaz with support from Iran, was the deadliest attack on U.S.

forces since the 1983 Beirut barracks bombing. It was a brutal reminder of the persistent threat of terrorism in the Middle East and the dangers faced by American troops stationed in the region.

Disney's Darkest Tale

Disney Studios continued its animation renaissance with the release of The Hunchback of Notre Dame on June 21. Based on Victor Hugo's classic novel, the film was noted for being one of Disney's darkest and most mature animated features. It dealt with complex themes of religious hypocrisy, sin, and social ostracism, and its villain, Judge Frollo, was one of the most complex and sinister in the Disney canon.

Conclusion: A Month of Contradiction

June was a month of powerful and contradictory emotions. The joy and celebration surrounding the Chicago Bulls' historic championship was a story of American excellence and dominance. But the tragic bombing at Khobar Towers was a painful and sobering story of American vulnerability. The month was a stark lesson in the complex realities of the time, where

moments of triumph could be instantly overshadowed by acts of tragedy.

Back to June memories

....

....

....

....

....

....

....

....

....

Picture of the month

06/1996

Back to
July
History

July

S	M	T	W	T	F	S
		1	2	3	4	5	6
7	8	9	10	11	12	13
14	15	16	17	18	19	20
21	22	23	24	25	26	27
28	29	30	31			

1996

A Flame of Hope, A Flash of Terror

July 1996 was a month where the celebratory spirit of the Olympic Games was tragically bookended by two shocking and devastating events. As the world gathered in Atlanta to celebrate athletic achievement, a mysterious plane crash off the coast of New York cast a pall of fear over the proceedings. And just days into the Games, that fear was realized when a terrorist's bomb ripped through a joyful crowd, turning a celebration into a scene of tragedy.

A Flame of Hope: The Atlanta Olympics Begin

On July 19, the Centennial Olympic Games opened in Atlanta, Georgia. The opening ceremony culminated in one of the most powerful and unforgettable moments in Olympic history. The identity of the final torchbearer had been a closely guarded secret. When the legendary boxer Muhammad Ali, the three-time heavyweight champion of the world, emerged into the stadium, the crowd roared. Visibly trembling from the effects of Parkinson's disease, Ali summoned all his strength and

courage to raise the torch and light the Olympic cauldron. It was a moment of immense dignity, bravery, and emotional power that transcended sport and moved a global audience to tears.

Tragedy Over the Atlantic: The Crash of TWA Flight 800

Just two days before the Olympic flame was lit, a terrible tragedy occurred. On July 17, TWA Flight 800, a Boeing 747 en route from New York to Paris, exploded and crashed into the Atlantic Ocean off the coast of Long Island. All 230 people on board were killed. The cause of the explosion was not immediately clear, and with the Olympics just about to begin, fears of a sophisticated terrorist attack were rampant. The crash triggered a massive investigation and a long, difficult recovery effort as search teams worked to retrieve the wreckage from the ocean floor. The mystery of TWA 800 would grip the nation for months.

Terror in the Park: The Centennial Olympic Park Bombing

The fears of terrorism were tragically realized on July 27. A pipe bomb, filled with nails and

screws, was left in a backpack underneath a bench in Atlanta's Centennial Olympic Park, a central gathering place for visitors and fans enjoying a free concert. The bomb exploded, killing one woman directly and injuring more than 100 others (a photojournalist also died of a heart attack while rushing to the scene). The death toll could have been much higher, but a security guard named Richard Jewell had discovered the suspicious package minutes before the blast and had begun clearing the area. In a cruel and unjust turn of events, Jewell, who was initially praised as a hero, was soon named by the media and the FBI as a primary suspect in the bombing. For months, he would be subjected to an intense and unfair trial by media before finally being exonerated.

A New Creation: Dolly the Sheep is Born

Away from the public eye, a quiet scientific revolution was underway. On July 5, at the Roslin Institute in Scotland, a lamb was born. Named Dolly, she was the first mammal to be successfully cloned from an adult somatic cell. While the news of her existence would be kept secret until the following year, her birth was a

monumental scientific milestone that would spark a fierce global debate on the ethics of cloning.

Conclusion: A Summer of Mixed Emotions

July was a month of jarring emotional whiplash. The inspirational opening of the Olympics was clouded by the mystery of a plane crash. The joy of the Games was then shattered by an act of domestic terrorism. The month was a difficult lesson in how celebration and tragedy can exist side-by-side, often separated by just a few moments in time.

Back to July memories

....

....

....

....

....

....

....

....

....

Picture of the month

07/1996

Back to
August
History

August

S	M	T	W	T	F	S
				1	2	3
4	5	6	7	8	9	10
11	12	13	14	15	16	17
18	19	20	21	22	23	24
25	26	27	28	29	30	31

1996

Building a Bridge: Conventions, Reform, and a New Superstar

August 1996 was the month the American presidential race moved into its final phase, with the two major parties holding their national conventions to officially nominate their candidates. In between the two conventions, President Bill Clinton made a bold and controversial move, signing a landmark bill that fundamentally reshaped the nation's social safety net. And in the world of sports, a young golf prodigy announced his arrival on the professional scene, a superstar destined to build his own kind of bridge to a new, more diverse era.

The Party Conventions

The political conventions of August set the stage for the fall campaign. From August 12 to 15, the Republican Party gathered in San Diego to formally nominate Senator Bob Dole of Kansas for president and former Congressman and football star Jack Kemp as his running mate. In contrast to the fiery "culture war" convention of 1992, the 1996 Republican

convention was a much more controlled and moderate affair, designed to present a more reassuring image to the nation.

Two weeks later, from August 26 to 29, the Democratic Party held its convention in Chicago. It was a triumphant and optimistic celebration, re-nominating the incumbent ticket of President Bill Clinton and Vice President Al Gore. The convention relentlessly pushed the theme of a strong economy and a nation moving in the right direction, using the slogan "Building a Bridge to the 21st Century" to frame the choice for voters.

The End of Welfare as We Know It

On August 22, President Clinton made one of the most consequential and controversial decisions of his presidency. He signed into law a sweeping welfare reform bill that had been passed by the Republican-controlled Congress. The "Personal Responsibility and Work Opportunity Act" fulfilled Clinton's campaign promise to "end welfare as we know it." The law ended the 61-year-old federal guarantee of cash assistance to the poor, placed a five-year lifetime limit on benefits, and required most

recipients to find work. The decision was hailed by conservatives and many moderates, but it was fiercely opposed by the liberal wing of the Democratic party, who saw it as a cruel betrayal of the nation's social safety net. The signing was a masterstroke of political "triangulation" that shored up Clinton's centrist credentials for the election.

"Hello, World": Tiger Woods Turns Pro

A new era in the world of golf, and sports marketing, began on August 27. Tiger Woods, the 20-year-old phenom who had just won his third consecutive U.S. Amateur championship, announced that he was turning professional. He began his press conference with the simple, now-iconic phrase, "Hello, world." The announcement was accompanied by the news that he had signed massive, multi-million dollar endorsement deals with Nike and Titleist before ever hitting a single shot as a pro. His arrival signaled the beginning of a new, more athletic, and more multicultural era for the sport he would go on to dominate.

A Royal Divorce is Finalized

The long and public saga of the Prince and Princess of Wales came to a final legal conclusion on August 28, when the divorce of Prince Charles and Princess Diana was officially finalized, formally ending their 15-year marriage.

Conclusion: Charting a Course for the Future

August was a month that clearly defined the political choice facing America. The two parties laid out their visions for the future, and President Clinton made a historic legislative gamble to claim the political center. As the Atlanta Olympics came to a close and the political campaigns kicked into high gear, the nation was fully engaged in the process of choosing the leader it wanted to build the bridge to the next century.

Back to August memories

....

....

....

....

....

....

....

....

....

Picture of the month

08/1996

Back to
September
History

September

S	M	T	W	T	F	S
1	2	3	4	5	6	7
8	9	10	11	12	13	14
15	16	17	18	19	20	21
22	23	24	25	26	27	28
29	30					

1996

A Voice Silenced, An Explosion Banned

September 1996 was a month of stark and tragic contrasts, a period that saw the violent silencing of one of the most powerful and prophetic voices in popular music, even as the nations of the world came together in a historic attempt to forever ban the sound of the most powerful explosions on Earth. The murder of a rap superstar and the signing of a global treaty against nuclear testing offered two very different and competing narratives about violence in the modern world.

The Death of a Rap Superstar: The Murder of Tupac Shakur

On the night of September 7, after attending a Mike Tyson boxing match in Las Vegas, rapper and actor Tupac Shakur was shot multiple times in a drive-by shooting as he sat in a car on the Las Vegas Strip. For six days, he fought for his life in a hospital. On September 13, he died from his injuries. He was 25 years old. The death of Tupac was a massive shock to the music world and to popular culture.

He was more than just a rapper; he was a complex, charismatic, and hugely influential figure whose music documented the rage, pain, and contradictions of life in modern urban America. His murder, which officially remains unsolved, became one of the most enduring mysteries in music history and elevated him to the status of a near-mythical figure.

A Ban on the Bomb: The Nuclear-Test-Ban Treaty

While one form of violence was dominating the headlines, the world's diplomats were working to end another. On September 24, the Comprehensive Nuclear-Test-Ban Treaty (CTBT) was opened for signature at the United Nations. The landmark treaty was designed to prohibit all nuclear explosions, for both military and civilian purposes, in all environments. President Bill Clinton was the first world leader to sign the treaty, and he was quickly followed by representatives from dozens of other nations, including the other major declared nuclear powers: Russia, the United Kingdom, France, and China. While the treaty would face a long and difficult path to ratification and has

never formally entered into force, its opening for signature was hailed as a major achievement of the post-Cold War arms control movement and a hopeful step toward a world free from the threat of nuclear testing.

The Nintendo 64 Arrives

A new front opened in the "console wars" of the 1990s. On September 29, the highly anticipated Nintendo 64 video game system was released in North America. With its powerful 64-bit processor and its innovative controller featuring an analog stick, the N64 offered a new level of 3D gaming. Its groundbreaking launch title, Super Mario 64, revolutionized the 3D platformer genre and is still considered one of the greatest video games ever made. The launch of the N64, which would compete directly with the Sony PlayStation and the Sega Saturn, was a major event in the world of home entertainment.

Missiles Over Iraq

A reminder of ongoing military conflict came early in the month. On September 3, the United States launched a series of cruise missile

strikes against military targets in southern Iraq. The strikes were a response to an Iraqi attack on a Kurdish safe haven in the north and were intended as a clear message to Saddam Hussein that the U.S. would continue to enforce the no-fly zones established after the Gulf War.

Conclusion: A Month of Contradictions

September was a month of deep contradictions. The murder of Tupac Shakur was a brutal story of real-world violence that seemed to confirm the dark narratives present in his own music. At the same time, the signing of the Nuclear-Test-Ban Treaty was a hopeful story of global cooperation aimed at ending the threat of nuclear violence forever. The month was a complex snapshot of a world struggling with its own violent impulses while simultaneously reaching for a more peaceful future.

Back to September memories

....

....

....

....

....

....

....

....

....

Picture of the month

09/1996

Back to October History

October

S	M	T	W	T	F	S
		1	2	3	4	5
6	7	8	9	10	11	12
13	14	15	16	17	18	19
20	21	22	23	24	25	26
27	28	29	30	31		

1996

The Power of the Screen: A New Network, A Final Debate, A Man's Exoneration

October 1996 was a month that powerfully demonstrated the immense and varied power of the television screen. A new cable news network was born that would change the American political conversation forever. A final presidential debate helped a national audience make its decision about who should lead the country. And a man who had been convicted in the court of television opinion was finally, officially, cleared, his story serving as a sobering cautionary tale about the destructive power of that same television screen.

A New Voice in News: The Launch of Fox News

On October 7, the American media landscape was permanently altered with the launch of the Fox News Channel. Created by media mogul Rupert Murdoch and run by the aggressive former Republican political strategist Roger Ailes, the 24-hour cable news network was founded with the slogan "Fair and Balanced."

It positioned itself as a conservative alternative to what it saw as a dominant liberal media establishment. While its initial reach was small, the launch of Fox News was a transformative event that would have a profound and lasting impact on the nature of American politics and journalism, contributing to the increasing polarization of the national discourse.

The Final Debates

The presidential race entered its final stretch with two televised debates between President Bill Clinton and his Republican challenger, Senator Bob Dole. The debates, held on October 6 and 16, solidified the dynamic of the race. President Clinton, enjoying a strong economy and a comfortable lead in the polls, appeared relaxed, confident, and full of detailed policy proposals for a "bridge to the 21st century." Senator Dole, by contrast, often seemed tired and struggled to articulate a clear and compelling reason for a change in leadership. The debates were widely seen as clear victories for Clinton, effectively ending any remaining suspense about the outcome of the election.

Richard Jewell is Cleared

For three months, he had been a household name for all the wrong reasons. Richard Jewell, the security guard who had discovered the bomb at the Centennial Olympic Park in July and helped to save lives, was quickly and wrongly identified by the media as the FBI's prime suspect in the attack. He was subjected to a relentless and overwhelming media stakeout, his life and reputation torn apart. On October 26, that ordeal finally came to an end. The U.S. Department of Justice delivered a letter to Jewell's attorneys formally and completely clearing him as a suspect. The exoneration was a vindication for Jewell, but it did not undo the immense damage that had been done. His story became a powerful and enduring lesson about the dangers of a media rush to judgment and trial by television.

Conclusion: A Media-Saturated World

October was a month whose biggest stories were all, in some way, about the media itself. A new news channel promised to change how people saw the world. A political debate shaped an election, and an innocent man's life was

ruined and then cleared, all in the full, unforgiving glare of the television lights. The month was a clear demonstration of the media's central and increasingly powerful role in shaping the realities of modern American life.

Back to October memories

....

....

....

....

....

....

....

....

....

Picture of the month

10/1996

Back to
November
History

November

S	M	T	W	T	F	S
					1	2
3	4	5	6	7	8	9
10	11	12	13	14	15	16
17	18	19	20	21	22	23
24	25	26	27	28	29	30

1996

A Bridge to the 21st Century: Clinton Wins a Second Term

November 1996 was the month the American electorate delivered a clear and decisive verdict. After a year of campaigning, voters chose to stay the course, re-electing President Bill Clinton by a comfortable margin and endorsing his optimistic vision for a "bridge to the 21st century." The election was a major personal triumph for a president who had suffered a devastating midterm defeat just two years earlier, and it confirmed the success of his strategy of leading from the political center.

The Re-Election of a President

On election day, November 5, President Bill Clinton defeated his Republican challenger, Senator Bob Dole. Clinton won a solid victory, capturing 379 electoral votes to Dole's 159 and winning nearly 49% of the popular vote in a three-way race with Reform Party candidate Ross Perot. The victory was historic: Clinton became the first Democrat to be elected to a second term since Franklin D. Roosevelt in 1944. His win was attributed to a number of

factors. The U.S. economy was strong and growing, with low unemployment and low inflation. Clinton had successfully co-opted major Republican issues like welfare reform and balancing the budget, positioning himself as a pragmatic "New Democrat." And the Dole campaign had struggled to present a compelling and forward-looking vision for the country. The election confirmed that Clinton's strategy of "triangulation" had been a resounding political success.

A New Mission to Mars

As the Clinton administration prepared for its second term, NASA was embarking on its own mission to the future. On November 7, the Mars Global Surveyor was launched from Cape Canaveral. The unmanned spacecraft was the first U.S. mission to be successfully launched to Mars in two decades. Its goal was to orbit the Red Planet and create a detailed map of its surface, beginning a new and highly successful era of Martian exploration.

Michael Jordan in Space: The Space Jam Phenomenon

The world's biggest sports superstar teamed up with the world's most famous cartoon characters in one of the year's biggest movie hits. On November 15, Space Jam premiered in theaters. The film starred basketball legend Michael Jordan playing himself, who is recruited by Bugs Bunny and the Looney Tunes to help them win a basketball game against a team of aliens who want to enslave them. The film's blend of live-action and animation, its massive star power, and its hit soundtrack made it a huge box office success and a pop culture touchstone for a generation of kids.

Tragedy Off the Comoro Islands

A dramatic hijacking ended in tragedy on November 23. Ethiopian Airlines Flight 961 was hijacked by three men seeking asylum in Australia. When the plane began to run out of fuel, the hijackers refused to let the pilot land. The plane eventually crashed into the Indian Ocean just off the coast of the Comoro Islands. Incredibly, the crash was caught on video by tourists on the beach. While 50 of the 175

people on board survived the water landing, 125 perished, making it one of the deadliest hijackings in history.

Conclusion: A Mandate for the Future

November was a month that delivered a clear mandate. By re-electing President Clinton, voters chose a path of continued economic growth and centrist problem-solving. With four more years in the White House secured, the president was now empowered to continue building his bridge to the new millennium, a journey that would soon be dominated by the challenges of the internet boom, global terrorism, and a series of domestic political scandals.

Back to November memories

....

....

....

....

....

....

....

....

....

Picture of the month

11/1996

Back to December History

December

S	M	T	W	T	F	S
1	2	3	4	5	6	7
8	9	10	11	12	13	14
15	16	17	18	19	20	21
22	23	24	25	26	27	28
29	30	31				

1996

Irrational Exuberance and an Unsolved Mystery

December 1996 was a month that perfectly captured the dual spirit of the late 1990s: a soaring, almost giddy economic optimism, and a dark, voyeuristic fascination with true crime and celebrity tragedy. The chairman of the Federal Reserve gave a name to the booming stock market's mood, while the mysterious death of a six-year-old child beauty queen in a wealthy Colorado home became a national obsession, a dark and unsettling mystery to end the year.

The Fed Chairman's Warning: "Irrational Exuberance"

The dot-com fueled stock market had been on a spectacular run, and by late 1996, some were beginning to worry it was a bubble. On December 5, the most powerful economic figure in the world gave voice to that anxiety. In a televised speech, U.S. Federal Reserve Chairman Alan Greenspan posed a now-famous rhetorical question about how to know when "irrational exuberance has unduly

escalated asset values." The phrase "irrational exuberance" was a carefully chosen piece of Fed-speak, a subtle warning that the central bank was concerned that the market was overheating. The financial world reacted instantly, with global stock markets briefly dipping. The phrase immediately entered the lexicon, perfectly capturing the giddy, and possibly baseless, optimism of the dot-com era.

A Horrible Mystery in Colorado: The Death of JonBenét Ramsey

On the day after Christmas, a horrific and bizarre crime story began to unfold in Boulder, Colorado. John and Patsy Ramsey, a wealthy couple, called 911 to report that their six-year-old daughter, JonBenét, had been kidnapped and that they had found a ransom note in their home. But just eight hours later, JonBenét's body was discovered in the basement of the house. She had been murdered. The case immediately became a massive media sensation. The combination of a wealthy family, a beautiful child who had participated in beauty pageants, and the strange circumstances of the crime created a media frenzy. The case, with its

many bizarre twists and turns, would become one of the most heavily publicized and enduring unsolved murder mysteries in American history.

A New Leader for the UN

The United Nations chose a new leader to guide it into the next century. On December 13, the Security Council selected Kofi Annan, a career diplomat from Ghana, to be the new Secretary-General. Annan, who had spent his entire career working within the UN system, was a respected and well-liked figure, and his selection was confirmed by the General Assembly a few days later.

A New Kind of Horror Movie

The horror movie genre, which had grown stale, was revitalized with the release of Scream on December 20. Directed by Wes Craven, the film was a clever, witty, and scary slasher film whose characters were fully aware of the clichés and "rules" of horror movies. Its self-referential humor and suspenseful plot made it a huge hit with audiences and critics, and it launched a new and successful horror franchise.

Conclusion: A Decade's Dual Nature

December was a month that held up a mirror to the dual nature of the late 1990s. "Irrational exuberance" perfectly described the booming economy and the feeling that the good times would never end. But the dark, unsettling, and endlessly publicized mystery of the JonBenét Ramsey case revealed a national obsession with tragedy, celebrity, and the dark secrets that can lurk behind a facade of wealth and perfection. The year ended with the nation feeling both incredibly prosperous and deeply unsettled.

Back to December memories

....

....

....

....

....

....

....

....

....

Picture of the month

12/1996

World History
What Happened in
1996
The Year You Were Born

- COST OF LIVING
- SPECIAL EVENTS
- SPORT EVENTS
- WORLD ECONOMY
- TECHNOLOGY
- POPULAR CULTURE